THE
OUTSKIRTS
OF TROY

OTHER BOOKS BY CARL DENNIS

A House of My Own
Climbing Down
Signs and Wonders
The Near World

THE OUTSKIRTS OF TROY

CARL DENNIS

William Morrow and Company, Inc., New York

Thanks are due to the editors of the following magazines, in which some of these poems, several in different versions, first appeared:

The Georgia Review, "Distance," "The List," and "Taking Both Sides";
Ironwood, "Guatemala," "The Party," "Summer Evening," and "At Becky's Piano Recital";
Michigan Quarterly Review, "Two Towns" (originally "The Meek");
The New Republic, "The Dig" (reprinted by permission, copyright © 1985);
The New Yorker, "On the Soul" (reprinted by permission, copyright © 1984);
Poetry, "The Dream of Fair Women," "Fairy Tales," "Fear of the Dark," "Heinrich Schliemann," "On the Way to School" (originally "The Matter of Troy"), and "The Spaniel" (originally "The Task");
Prairie Schooner, "Visiting a Friend Near Sagamon Hill" (originally "Fenton Road");
Salmagundi, "Henry James and Hester Street" and "The Promised Land";
The Sonora Review, Part III of "Twenty Years" (originally "A Page from Greenhaven Prison") and "The Mood";
Virginia Quarterly Review, "Governors and Priests" and "Voice Lessons."

Part I of "Twenty Years" and "The Dream of Fair Women" first appeared in *The Breadloaf Anthology of Contemporary Literature,* edited by Robert Pack, Sydney Lea, and Jay Parini (Hanover and London, 1985).

I also want to thank the Guggenheim Foundation for a grant that provided the leisure during which some of these poems were written.

Finally, I want to express my gratitude to the friends who read these poems, sometimes in several versions, and gave me indispensable criticism: Charles Altieri, Alan Feldman, Leonard Nathan, Martin Pops, Donald Revell, Philip Schultz, and Burton Weber.

Library of Congress Cataloging-in-Publication Data

Dennis, Carl.
    The outskirts of Troy / Carl Dennis.
        p. cm.
    ISBN 0-688-07755-2.   ISBN 0-688-07756-0 (pbk.)
    I. Title.
PS3554.E53509 1988
811'.54—dc19   87-22881
                                                                    CIP

Printed in the United States of America

First Edition

1 2 3 4 5 6 7 8 9 10

BOOK DESIGN BY BARBARA MARKS

For Charles Altieri

CONTENTS

I

HENRY JAMES AND HESTER STREET

Two or three characters talking in a lamplit parlor
Beside a fire, the curtains closed—
So the novel begins, and James is happy.
What a relief to reach this quiet shelter,
Back from America, far from the castles of Fifth Avenue,
From their fresh, unweathered vulgarity,
Far from change run wild, the past trundled away,
His father's dependable neighborhood
Forced to give ground to "glazed perpendiculars"
That compel the passers-by to feel equal, equally small.

In the curtained parlor, where tea is being served,
The banker protagonist fills the cups so graciously
I'm convinced he's gathered his treasure with spotless
    hands,
His flaws as fine as the hairline cracks
In the landscapes from the Renaissance that adorn the
    walls.
Why shouldn't James protect his characters from the
    world
If that's what he thinks they need to be free?
Soon they'll have problems enough of their own
Without being made to feel what their maker felt
Touring Manhattan slums, shoved to the curb
By hordes of "ubiquitous aliens." Imagine those crowds
Hawking and bargaining on Hester Street,
Their clanging pushcarts and swarming children,
Immigrants like the couple in the photograph in my hall,
My mother's father and mother fresh off the boat.
Had I stood where James stood back then
They'd have made me uneasy too,

Though now I assume they felt even more alien
Than James felt when he left for good.

As the banker, setting his cup down,
Peers at a landscape to inspect some travelers
Sheltered under a plane tree in a storm,
I inspect the faces in the photograph
As they stare out, eager and sober,
Brave though confused. Their faith in a life
Whose outlines even now are still concealed
Inspires me, just as James's fidelity to his muse
Must have inspired the younger writers who visited.
Pulling their coats on, they stepped out into the chill
And grimy fog they planned to describe in plainer,
Ruder detail, but in a light more revealing
Than the murky light of history, the day more mean-
    ingful
Than any November Tuesday in 1913.

THE MOOD

Before I open my eyes I hear the rain
Banging on a metal lid in the driveway,
The sound of a gong in a country temple.
In my mind's eye I can almost make out the monks
Seated in their orange robes in the prayer room
Waiting for love from the great void
To release them gently from their own will
And choose them as its eager vehicle.

When it fails to come to my bed,
Something gentle in the air this morning
Lets me hope at least that others are inspired,
That they forgive the friend who's left them
And do it with an eagerness I've never shown,
That they try to imagine what she feels
As she watches the rain blowing across the road.

The rain rinses the window of my study
As I skim the headlines. No time while the mood lasts
To linger on a case of kickbacks in Washington.
Better the story of the local rich man
Who willed the funds for the library roof repair
When he himself was too busy to read.
Better to praise the few at the rainy reopening
Who gathered on the steps to sing.

In the rain-washed light of the photograph
The singers appear mild and luminous,
Citizens of a country not yet explored
That never breaks its treaties with the Indians,

Never steals an inch from Mexico,
That is faithful to its many gods.

Rocking on the porch at nightfall, eyes closed,
I smell in the wind blowing from their fields
The pungent groves sacred to Fortune
Close by the smaller groves of Justice and Liberty.
No rich man there believes he's earned his forests.
No poor man interprets his empty potato sack
As a sign that plenty has arrived
In some other district that deserves it more.

THE LIST

How the frail, shimmering hollyhocks
Share in a bloom that's deathless and invisible—
That was the question that kept students awake,
Chewing their quills in the old school,
Staring at the blank pages of diaries.
How much simpler for me to make my list
Of every shimmering, dying thing I come across.
Rainy West Delham Street gets a line
And rain-washed Ellicott Elementary School
With the puddles in the schoolyard,
And the sunrise on the flags of the car lot,
And the cars themselves, dozing in the shadows.

As for the beautiful moments,
Why should I wait around anymore
For the sidewalk to part like the Red Sea
Or the painter's ladder to fill with angels,
Visions that prove the world a dream?
The moments that make the world seem real
Are all I need now. I can add to my list
The foggy morning when the children next door
Woke me with a trumpet fanfare.
I can add this evening's walk with Karen to the dock
And our comments on last night's movie,
What exactly went wrong with it.
We make the confusions of ugly art beautifully clear
By the time we pause at the tracks
To count the boxcars, close to a hundred,
All sporting the rust I noticed as a boy.
They've almost dropped their pretense of utility.
Their rattling by again seems part of a ritual
To make us feel at home,
And maybe it will work this time
If I don't imagine us welcomed elsewhere,
Counting the boxcars in another world.

HEINRICH SCHLIEMANN

If the main plot in his life were his rise
From grocer's apprentice and shipwrecked scrivener
To rich indigo merchant with a palace in St. Petersburg,
The master of a dozen languages, it would be easy
For critics like us to patronize,
Easy to grant him a place in the storybook
With Dick Whittington and the woodcutter's youngest
    son.
And we could pity his distance from the real world
When he leaves the trading firm in middle age
To learn the ancient Greek of Homer
And falls in love with an Athenian schoolgirl
As he hears her recite Andromache's long plea
And marries her, moving his life from storybook
Into dream, as if the noise of traffic outside the church
Were the hubbub on the fields around Troy.

If only he hadn't taken it into his head
To dig in a sleepy backwater village
For Troy's walls and somehow found them;
If he hadn't knelt in the dirt all day
With beautiful Sophia, chipping away crust
From the tiles of Priam's palace, from bracelets
That once circled the slim wrists of princesses;
If he hadn't proved that his dream was graspable,
That the stories he loved were fashioned in the high style
Not to escape the world but to remember it,
An offering to the dead, to the dead bright ones
Whose gestures, vivid as they are in song,
Were doubtless in the flesh more dazzling.

SNOW GEESE

In the South they find all the grain they need,
In winter as well as spring and fall.
So you'd think summers down there would be a carnival
And they'd choose to spare themselves the toil
Of flying north ten thousand miles
To breed and nest and fatten their young
In the few rushed weeks before the lakes freeze.

Maybe it's true that once, when the earth was warmer,
They lived in the Arctic all year long,
That June pulls them to return to their old home.
More proof that the past can weigh the living down
With habits reason alone can free us from.

"This is the way we've always done things;
This is what it means to be a snow goose,"
They cry, as they fly back to the motherland,
No genuine pioneer among them.
No one like the man waving good-bye
One morning to Sumer or Babylon,
Poling his raft upriver into wilderness,
Bringing lamps and plank floors to caves,
Rakes and hammers, jars and brooms,
For a town he plans to give his name to.

I hear them flying in their grooved path
Over the new wing of my house,
Over the windows I've widened to let more light in
And the porch I've moved ten feet to the west
For an ampler view of the snowy mountains,
Hoping the vista inspires me with more calm

Or more ambition, more pride or humility,
Depending on the moods I choose to live by

And the need my species is born with
For freedom and control and harmony,
Need I haven't studied as I should.
I'm free to work against it, as the geese are not,
Just as I'm free to pluck my right eye out
If it offend me and call myself
A seeker of a truer life, pilgrim, pioneer,
Whatever name I choose for a one-eyed man.

TWO TOWNS

"Four hours of work here,"
Says the one mechanic in the town
Where my car dies, so I stroll the streets,
Streets so quiet and drab
I wonder if I've come to the home
Inherited by the meek.
Maybe this brown they've painted their houses with
Is really their favorite color,
Not chosen from timidity,
Brown fearlessly drab
Through which they make their statement about earth
    tones,
About the earth they're not sorry to be a part of,
Not afraid to return to and mix with.

Back home in the city,
At the dinner I'm missing out on,
Where my friend pouring the wine
Wonders what's held me up,
They're talking about books that last,
The ones true to the way things stand
In the durable light beyond appearances
Where the diners would also like to stand but can't
Though no one denies they deserve more
Than the years a stingy fate allots them.

Here I imagine a housewife pausing in the kitchen
Midway in the recipe for the peach pie her son enjoys
To listen to the wind as it bangs the house boards,
Glad she didn't wait for a day of celebration.
Only if I give the boy sweeping the front steps
My longings does he look unsatisfied,
Troubled that his talent on the violin

Won't ever be developed beyond a sideline,
Won't ever be heard in concert by my friends,
Who now, as they finish off their desserts,
May be comparing timeless performances.

A shame that their talk isn't written down
For future generations, that soon they'll remember
Only the usable residue
While the delicate fragrance of the hour
Will have blown off.
I can see the friend who's kept my chair free
Holding his wine to the light to test the amber
As if nature and art for this brief moment
Are on trial. An impromptu lesson
In grasping the hour as it flakes away
To sprinkle the brown earth,
Earth that fails to value the costly gift
As no god should fail, no god worth worshiping.

FEAR OF THE DARK

Fear of the dark stays with me but not the shame.
And the worry that my story won't reach the light
Where other stories wait and be understood
No longer seems a weakness I should overcome.

So what if it does to others, to the few who require
Only themselves to fill their theaters. For them
It's a mystery why even Hamlet, no lover of the world,
Is anxious, dying, for the world to get the facts right

And makes Horatio promise to retell the play;
Why even the dead in Hell cry out to Dante
To carry their stories back; why Dante,
Banished from Florence, promises.

No need for anyone who doesn't ask to be heard
To hear the dead of Sodom crying for an audience
Though it's likely some good men died in that fire,
Fathers to widows and orphans, friends to the poor.

After the ashes settled, the scribes blackened the name
Of the charred walls to keep God's name pure.
It won't be easy to say enough
To get those ghosts to rest in the dark

As Troy rests, its ashes content with Homer's account
Of its long war and fiery fall,
Beautiful Troy, city beloved of Zeus,
Whose altars day and night smoked with offerings.

II

DISTANCE

The old man across the courtyard,
Reading alone in his window seat,
Looks like a real student
Awed by the vision and honesty of a page
When over here he might look bored or lonely.

If the woman at the door this evening
Who asked for my signature
Had knocked over there,
She wouldn't have looked as she did,
Harried merely, and graying, and fat,
With a son and daughter behind her
Squabbling over a toy.

Even here, had I stood back far enough,
Her speech on the arms race and covert wars
Would have sounded serious.
Now that she's passed from sight
With the long view her neighbors refuse to take,
I try to imagine her in the distance arriving home.
By now she's hanging the three coats in the hall
Beside the landscapes her children painted in school,
Which look no brighter to her
Than the ones she did herself thirty years back,
The same dragons and swampy woods.

She'll have to stand back farther
To imagine how the paintings might look one day
With their dark hues brighter,
Their fears cast out.
Whatever helps her to see that far
Is a power I should try now to explore.
I should think about why it behaves this way,

Giving her yearnings that the present can't satisfy,
Not even the present, silent world
Of the people across the courtyard,
Beyond the endless arguments of last week
That people over here are still repeating.

GUATEMALA

Till Guatemala came up,
Each of us sitting in the yard last night
Was eager to have his say, whatever the topic.
One glance at the stars was enough
To set us musing about destiny:
How we're free at least to journey where our thoughts
    lead,
How the hope to find our conclusions seconded by the
    skies
Is only a child's wish for a night light.

And when the wind blew right,
We caught the music from a yard party in the neigh-
    borhood.
How wonderful, we said, the things people do
To inscribe the empty stretch of the year with punctua-
    tion:
Dances and birthday recitals, parades and planting fes-
    tivals,
The dawn songs one of us heard years ago in Guatemala
When the Indians still felt like singing.

That's when the talk faltered. It seemed crude
To mention that ruined country without lingering.
It seemed foolish to waste our time with the obvious:
Why the few landowners refuse to share,
Why they'd rather thin the Indians out like deer.
Greed is merely greed,
A subject covered already in Sunday School
With the Fall of Man and Original Sin.
And who needs another example of human stupidity
On a grand scale, a refusal to look ahead one day?
Why dwell on the wide-eyed looks in Washington

When it's learned the Indians see us as the enemy
For ousting the one leader who took their side?

It cramps the soul to think about it too long.
We shouldn't have blamed ourselves
For wanting to climb from the smoke of the underworld
And gulp the breath of earth, the sweeet night air.
One of us should have remarked how far the stars
    looked,
How glad he was to know they hadn't been made
In the heart's image but lived apart,
Indifferent and impervious.
Then our talk might have begun again.

TO A FRIEND OFF TO TEACH
FOR A YEAR IN RUSSIA

Kenny's rabbi wants to know if you have room
For these three prayer books for the Moscow synagogue.
And here's a packet of letters from an émigré friend
To his relatives in Kostroma.
Mailed from Moscow, they might get through.

For myself, I've only a few titles
I think you should start your classes with,
Moby Dick on top, though its nautical terms
Will doubtless slow your students down.
They like big novels over there, remember,
Epics that wrestle, win or lose, with the big questions.
Ahab's dividing the world into two powers,
The good one weak and homeless, the dark enthroned,
Could lead you naturally to today's myth
Of Satan's empire, that both sides seem trapped in.

Then to expose the myth you hate the most,
That the state is a god worthy our final sacrifice
And not a servant, I'd turn to Emerson
Though your students will resist the myth he loves
That man himself is a god or a god in ruins.
Let them. Encourage them.
Don't try to control the discussion too much.
Don't impose a thesis if you have one.
Imitate Ishmael, not so entangled in the plot
That he can't step back and digress, a free man.

Waiting in vain for a label to pin on you,
The party faithful will doze off at their desks,
Allowing your real students to ask what worries them:
Why, if America is a free country,

Do its leaders seem no wiser than their own,
With the same schemes to topple democracies
That don't seem friendly enough, and to prop up Cae-
    sars?
Can the countrymen of a seer like Whitman,
Who glances from Brooklyn to India in a single line,
Lift their eyes no farther than their paychecks?

However much you concede then, don't waste class time
Teaching satiric novels with tiny
Suburban characters undone by sloth.
Better the adventure of a whaling ship
Staved in by a whale.
Your students won't be coming to class to mock.
They'll want to know if Ahab is justified
In his outrage that he's not more powerful.
They'll want to agree with you after weeks of wrangling
On the meaning that the wreck might have
To the one character who manages to return,
How exactly, though he's still uncertain,
He's wiser than he was before.

IN THE REPUBLIC

Bright as the morning is,
The schoolteacher awakening now
Over the lamp store on Wabash Street
Is certain it isn't a real day,
That the gust lifting his curtains
Hasn't blown in from a real dawn.

How can he tell
Unless he's been shown the pattern
That the dawns of the world are copied from?
One glimpse of the sun Plato describes
And then the twilight of earth
And his efforts merely to survive in style,
His wardrobe adjusted to the weather report,
The weather an image of the repetition of history
His country points to as progress,
As the march of fate.

Here comes another chapter to tire him
With cheaper land in the West,
Timber and railroads, cotton, cattle, gold,
Ships with the biggest holds
Steaming into foreign harbors
Till the time comes to lose their trade
To ships loaded with merchandise
Cheaper than ours, to watch the armadas of Taiwan
Pass on their endless patrols around the world.

In the country that time brings him no closer to
The students would be reminded of the real light
By the light that now pours through the window,
As bright as it's ever been,

The sun untroubled by the dark fate
Of other mornings freely bestowed.

Can this school at the corner of Walnut and Hodge
With the asphalt playground really be a school
Where the rulers of the just republic are trained?
Can the students learn from the chubby man
In the reindeer sweater and suede shoes
To choose from the pile of episodes only the real ones
And weave them into a story of their own
Truer than a chronicle, simple as a song?

SUMMER EVENING

They're pleasant-looking, these couples and foursomes
Chatting in quiet tones this evening in the Beanstalk,
Sunday, July 20, 1986,
Five days after the All-Star Game,
Three weeks after the House vote to sponsor a war
Against Nicaragua. In the light of hooded candles,
In soft shadows, their eyes are warm.
They look like believers who made a vow in church
This morning to renounce the settling of old scores,
Who've made peace with their enemies.
Now they're feeling happy enough with themselves
To go home to the quiet sleep they deserve
While the fretful sleep of many in Washington
Is broken by nightmares of Nicaragua at work
Building a wooden horse too wide for our boulevards
Or burning a sacrifice to the gods of plague.
Any nightmare that worried these diners in childhood
Seems to have vanished years back with the trolls
Who waited under their beds for the lights to dim.
Reason won out, reason and their patient teachers
Who broke up the fistfights at recess and called them in
To study the end of the Dark Ages, the expanding trade
    routes,
The blossoming of the arts, the voyages of discovery,
The settling of New England, the long push west
That left in its wake West Hodge Street and the Beanstalk
Humming now with the conversation of citizens
Who've voted to stop inflation,
Lower taxes, and get their jobs back.
No slouches either when it comes to digging deep
In their pockets for the orphanage or the school band.
They'd dig deep now for Nicaragua
If only it could appear before their tables

In the guise of a waitress whose lips are bruised,
A cook whose arms are scarred from grease burns,
A father outside the window, standing by his steaming
    U-Haul,
Taking his troubles out on a girl
Stupid enough to be born to losers.
Now it's only a name in the paper
Of a country they've never visited
Caught up in what's called a tragedy.
The plot is confusing even to the chorus on stage
As messengers crowd into Thebes.
How can these citizens feasting in the Beanstalk
Be clattering to the place where three roads meet
To quarrel with a stranger on the right of way?

TO A FRIEND CONCERNING
AMERICA'S SUPPORT FOR
THE DICTATORSHIP IN CHILE

Useful on this Election Day
To remind yourself you inhabit here
Nothing so impersonal as a state,
That what you feel cut off from
Are only the few people in power
And the many who freely chose them,
Fellow Americans who can stroll,
Chatting, to the polling place
Not followed by police,
Not deafened by tanks rumbling over cobblestones.

Useful today when you're feeling powerless
In a country you can't believe you ever believed in
To remember that few waiting in line here
Would be friendly to a foreign power
Unfriendly to its citizens
If they could climb a watchtower
And see how the sky looks over there
In a prison with no visiting days.
And what would it take for them to notice our ships
Riding at anchor in those harbors
But a willingness to distrust the leaders
They're waiting in line to elect again,
To distrust the charm of the homely polling place,
The school gym festooned for the fall dance,
The social hall of the church ready for the bake sale.

Gratitude is the way they prove to themselves
They're loving daughters and loyal sons.
And can't you say, as you wait among them,
That you feel like a son as well
If many countries make you angry
But only one makes you poor and small?

GOVERNORS AND PRIESTS

When the story came to light about our governor,
How he lined his pockets selling pardons to prisoners,
He kept on selling them, unashamed. Fifty-two
On one night in his last week in office. A record.

Knowing the law of averages, we escaped much of the
    shame
Priests felt when the popes sold indulgences.
If ten per cent of Caesar's servants are corruptible,
Ten per cent of the Caesars can't resist for long.

The good news is his being discovered and forced out.
A woman hired to skew the books blew the whistle in-
    stead,
Proof that the system sometimes works after all
And can cure itself, like the church, given enough time.

The only harm done, besides the freeing of a few crooks,
Was to make the new wardens nervous.
They could use some help in telling the remorseful crimi-
    nals
From the frauds, could use a priest or two
If any could be spared now from parish jobs.

You can't blame the new governor in these days
Of a priest shortage for being extra cautious.
Sad to pass by the shuttered windows of the seminary
And think of blinkered parole boards, their wary igno-
    rance,

Their worry at not getting enough respect, deciding to
    keep back
The silent, unbowing candidate for five more years.

And could you blame a priest for not choosing the job?
Who would want to work so far from the sun?
The men he'd admire would be just the ones
Maimed most by the dark they lived in.
And imagine having the old governor in your flock.
Imagine listening every day to his one regret:
Trusting that bitch who spilled the beans.

Time for those who believe in saints
To reread the story of St. Francis.
His belief that even the birds had souls
Was heresy to the church.
They made him a saint anyway. Why?
Unless they needed him as an antidote
To priests who assumed nobody was out there,
Nobody in the troubled silence, listening.

THE PROMISED LAND

The land of Israel my mother loves
Gets by without the luxury of existence
And still wins followers
Though it can't be found on the map
West of Jordan or south of Lebanon,
Though what can be found bears the same name,
Making for confusion.

Not the land I fought her about for years
But the one untarnished by the smoke of history,
Where no one informs the people of Hebron or Jericho
They're squatting on property that isn't theirs,
Where every settler can remember wandering.

The dinners I spoiled with shouting
Could have been saved,
Both of us lingering quietly in our chairs,
If I'd guessed the truth that now is obvious,
That she wasn't lavishing all her love
On the country that doesn't deserve so rich a gift
But on the one that does, the one not there,
That she hoped supplies could reach its borders
And hopes they're crossing even now

Into the land of the righteous and merciful
That the Prophets spoke of in their hopeful moods,
That was loved by the red-eyed rabbis of Galicia
Who studied every word of the book and prayed
To get one thread of the meaning right;
The Promised Land where the great and small
Hurry to school and the wise are waiting.

TWENTY YEARS

for John Hemmers

I

Other prisoners you've written to
Must have told you stories like mine,
How, when they were ten or eleven,
Their fathers began to drink too much,
How when the beatings grew too heavy
They ran loose all night.

I'm willing to admit that my brothers, as wild as I was,
Turned out all right. I don't compare
Their daily killings on the market now
With the one killing on my hands.

All I ask you to see is how much more hate
I had to keep in check than you had to
Or have to now, how good feelings,
When they come to you, come mostly from the heart,
Unforced, not from the will.
If I could write well
I'd write a book on the subject of unequal chances,
Unequal tests and trials,
And not mention myself at all.

The subject must interest you too.
Why else would you want to write me,
A stranger and a prisoner? I'm glad you do
In spite of the days when a bad taste rises in my throat
As I think how little anger you have to swallow

Waking each day in the sunlit, carpeted room
I imagine you waking in.
It's a full day's work for me not to envy
Your lack of envy for any man
As you look down on your garden.

In my best daydream I see myself down there
Talking with your friends, nodding and laughing.
I'm cheering on a friendly game of croquet
And want to join in, but don't,
Afraid that the mallet in my hands
Might turn out dangerous, a missed shot
Stirring up something dark from the bottom
That for years had been slowly settling
Because I'd been holding my life still.

II

Now that they're sleeping,
Their radios still till dawn,
I'm alone with the thin wedge of stars
Visible from the high window.
I have time to name all the clusters I can,
Trying to move with them as they shift west
Over land I want to know more of,
Old free states and slave,
Indian settlements, abandoned mining camps.

The more I learn, the more I feel wasted here
And the lonelier, angry at the many
Not angered by their ignorance,
Then angry at myself for vanity.
Why should they want to study
When the only student they know
Is far more sullen than they are

And aging faster, gray as a ghost,
The thinnest shadow in the land of shadows.

III

Yesterday wind seemed to be blowing
Out through the open gate of the garden
I try to believe in,
The one I carry with me.
I could almost smell the trees blossoming.
And it seemed that nothing here could hurt me.
Whatever happened would leave me strong,
Whatever time did or the guards.
And the guards seemed human,
Even the worst ones, more afraid than cruel.

So if today the wind carries no garden smell,
Should I believe I dreamed it
Any more than I dreamed the world,
The slums and mud flats,
The pear tree I once shook pears from?
Among the hours of hate, I can clear a space
For simple sorrow to breathe in.
When I find in a guard's face nothing I want to find,
I must imagine what he might have
    been,
The boy on the street on summer evenings
Playing hard at hide-and-go-seek,
Cheering as a friend scrambles across the lawn
To the home tree to free the prisoners.

IV

The world locks us away and forgets,
But we never forget the world.
And if you can come on diploma day,
You can watch the few men in the study program

Receive their scrolls in the visiting room,
Students of earth crust and epics,
Foreign policy, light refraction,
Roman history, the food chain.
You can see them in the honors block
Watching the evening news.

You'd be surprised how few laugh
When the President says that America
Will ignore the World Court for the next two
    years,
How many feel ashamed for him
As they walk back to their cells
To daydream in the hour before bed
That their crime is undone,
That a woman is lying on the cot with them
And the cot is a blanket under the stars.

Last month I sent you my thoughts on Jefferson.
This month I'm reading Russian thinkers.
I love the way they resist regret
And look ahead as Jefferson does
To a new order, with justice for all,
No masters and no slaves, no wars or colonies.
Were they studied today
By those with power in Moscow or Washington
More countries would be free now
And appeals wouldn't be piling up in the mailrooms.

I imagine a clerk in a hall of the Great Powers
Sorting the letters into piles:
This pile from those unwilling to take the long view
About hardship in the provinces, about vital interests;
This pile from those who'd send the wrong signal

To the enemy, who'd make us appear weak
By backing down.

No need for me to reread your words
To make me wonder what your life is like
And hope if you need help that help is coming,
Rumbling through the night by the truckload.
Meanwhile I can tell from here
How the letters in the Great Hall are hauled off
By the truckload to be burned,
How the smoke near the dump is so thick
The neighbors complain in letters to the authorities.

V

I'll be all right when I get out of here
If I don't look back to wonder who I might have been
Had I never been locked away
And don't live fast, trying to make the years up.

Even here I've done what I could with books
To climb above the wall and guard towers
And look out over trees I can't touch
Down through house windows and screen doors.
I can almost see the people sitting down to eat:
The happy ones easy to believe in
And the sad ones no more comforted by their
     paintings
Than I am by my iron bed
Or my steel sink and toilet bowl.

And when the guards yell at me to come down,
I don't allow my anger to flare out
As I strain to catch the talk in the dining room.
And if the cries of the boy I was
Rise to my lookout, I don't look back on his beatings,

And lament. I climb higher, so high
Even the sobs of the grown man for the boy
Can't reach me.

Like the sailors in the story
With wax stuffed in their ears, not like the hero,
I sail by, and my ship isn't turned toward home.
The future must contain what I haven't seen
In a place I've never visited
If it's holding something good in store for me.

III

THE DREAM OF FAIR WOMEN

Once when they came to my bed in dream,
They came in the dark, nameless, bodies only.
Then they came in the light, faces visible,
Faces of women I could hope to encounter soon
If my luck changed, if I played my cards right,
Docked on the right islands,
My face bronzed from the sea sun.
Now they come as the few women I've known well.

Is this a sign of the change I'm most afraid of,
The slow shifting of hope to memory?
They don't return as I remember them,
But older, as they might look now,
Their foreheads lined, dark hair crowded by gray.
One day their youth got up before dawn
And left them sleeping, and they woke up serious,
Not mournful, and saw from their window
That the mainland they called their home
Was in fact an island
With a single harbor seldom used.

In the waystation of my bed,
Their hands gripping my shoulders,
They tell their stories, saved up
Voyage after voyage for ears like mine.
However I listened before,
In my dream I listen carefully.
As I wake the words fade
But the tone lingers, which is all I need
To know what stories of my own are true.

KITCHEN WINDOW

A mistake to blame my neighbor whose wife is dying
For raking leaves with the same attention to detail
He's always shown for his yard, careful as always
To sweep the birdbath clean and shake the bushes.
Nothing wrong in his reasoning
That what brought pleasure before,
A clearer glimpse of finches and warblers,
Might bring a little distraction now.

And nothing wrong when the birds fade out
In turning for help to a movie on TV,
One that tries to deny death the last word
When its heroine is dragged down,
Closing instead with a shot of her son
Reading in her diary of a day long gone
When she still felt well enough to stroll the fields,
Her friends beside her,
And found, for an afternoon, pure joy.

And when the movie fails to satisfy,
Let him turn to a novel that dismisses time as a dream,
That begins at the end and works backward,
Chapter by chapter, to the earliest hours.
Slowly the dead come back to life, the old grow young,
Scattered children return to their first home,
To parents with unblemished vows,
And sing the songs forgotten in Chapter One.

Is this a trick, my neighbor wonders,
Or does a truth hide in the method somewhere
Waiting to be explored?
Maybe it's better to rake leaves, to sit up,
While his wife sleeps, to watch the news,

Wondering why the wars in Africa and Afghanistan,
The earthquakes and plane disasters,
Don't seem more real.

The real program worth waiting up for
Would be a message beamed from a far-off galaxy,
Some encouragement from planets wiser than ours.
Who can imagine it? By the time it arrives
The senders will be dead a thousand years,
Their words, whatever they offered at first
In the way of promise,
Shrunk down to "Friend, remember me."

FAIRY TALES

There's still time, before the scribe sits down,
For you to saddle your horse
And ride to the glass mountain
And find the princess spellbound in the ice.
All you need are the coral horseshoes from the island.
Why must the one to fetch them be the shoemaker's son,
Who's still a child, sitting in his parents' house,
Reading sea stories?
By day he's an apprentice in your bindery,
To you merely another shirker,
Lingering out his lunch hour on the hill
Above the harbor, watching the sails.
You signed him on as a favor to his mother,
The sweetheart of your boyhood,
And now you're sorry. No gratitude there.
Another annoyance to be listed in your diary
Beside the list of adventures that might have been yours
In a country with more freedom and sympathy.

When the boy asks permission to go to sea
You can almost sympathize. When he's ready to leave
Without permission you wear old man's clothes.
Soon from your window you spy the new-made prince
And rescued princess riding by,
Festooned with flowers. One glance makes clear
You'd have loved her better than he ever will,
A raw boy with no experience,
No means to understand what a prize he has.
Now you'll have to play uncle at the wedding feast.
When they call you for a toast
You'll be tempted to say something so wise
The princess will regret it wasn't your kiss
That broke the spell. But what good is that now,

To see her pensive, to trade knowing looks in church
Year after year, brooding on what might have been?
Better to toast the crowd with a story
That includes them all, you and the princess,
The horseshoes, your bustling bindery,
Your old flame, the harbor, the prince on the hill.
All woven together just as they really were
But with the rarity emphasized.
Few will believe it could happen as it did
Unless the characters magically willed it all
From the beginning, unknown to themselves,
And would will it now, again and again,
You and the others, you most of all.

THE PARTY

The woman in the blue dress might have listened harder
To my notions about land reform—why so far,
In countries to the south of us, it's gotten nowhere,
Why America seems as afraid of change
As Rome was at the ebb of the Empire—
If I hadn't let my voice rise to a shout,
Leading her to interpret my big, impersonal grief
As a small and private one,
As a belated rebellion, say, against my father,
From which she wasn't likely to learn much.

Safer to expound on countries farther off
In the world of what might have been.
She'd have enjoyed my theory about Alexander,
What might have happened if instead of marching east
To conquer Asia he'd chosen more wisely to march west,
Leaving among tribes half wild
A string of outposts to the Pillars of Hercules.

How can we know what we really are,
I'd have asked for, or what world we live in,
Unless we try to imagine what we've lost,
Which is everything except what we have now.

Just think of praying to sky gods,
Our wishes rising through the clouds in Greek
While the army of Buffalo drills in the agora
And the ships of foreign ambassadors
Sail up the Niagara to the villa of the mayor.

She wouldn't have had to worry in that republic
About spoiling her children, whether it's wrong
To ask them what they'd like for supper

Or to let them play long after nightfall.
Indulgence would be part of a plan to train heroes,
To get them to see the world as theirs,
As a field for chasing after the beautiful.

And if she asked me then what should be done
If they chase after something like wealth or power,
The cheers of the ignorant, the glory of empire,
If all her inspired arguments flutter brightly
Over their heads unrecognized, and out the window,
And down the road to the graveyard,

I'd tell her she should try to imagine herself
Watching the action unfold
As one of the chorus of advisers in a tragedy,
Free of the rancor that the young are mired in,
Free of confusion and quarreling.
Their hearts are clear
As they reach a decision on the next step
That the hero would be sure to take
If someone could make him listen
And he knew what was good for him.

VOICE LESSONS

So your voice rings hollow.
So it echoes like a shout in a grand hotel
Built near Pigeon River to attract the railroad,
Forty-five rooms and each one empty.

Why not think of yourself
As an infant Cleveland, Milwaukee, or St. Paul,
A raw scatter of cabins in the wilderness
With a printing press unloaded at a log wharf
And dragged through a drizzle to a leaky tent?
The first newspaper that's run off
Is a booster advertisement for another Eden
Complete with factories, schools, and hospitals
Soon to be built if not already begun.

All lies, but lies that could turn out true
If enough people believe them
And steam in on the packet boat
And run to the tent to list their services:
Tooth-puller, saddle-maker, seller of dry goods.

Whoever you want to be is the truer part
Of your nature, more resistant to time
Than the habits you happen to practice now,
Which you have no reason to admire,
No duty to be loyal to.

Let the rude family of travelers
Stamp on the floor for service.
Let them complain the beds are lumpy,
The floors shaggy with splinters,
The windows nailed shut and painted over

With vague vistas of domes and spires
Soaring over rainbow crowds.

Let them grumble at your singing
As you dawdle on the stairs.
Give yourself to the songs not learned by listening
To rumors from the world of stumps and mud.

ACCIDENT ON THE BRIDGE

I'd be there now, waving in the depot
As my aunt's train pulls in,
If the pie truck, taking the turn to the bridge too fast,
Hadn't rolled on its side, spilling pies,
Blocking the way as effectively as a swamp would
Or a forest in a stretch of serious narrative
Where the hero can't get back to the threatened town.

Now my aunt will be making excuses for me
As she's done for many others in her life,
People I never wanted to be compared to.

Now she might be consoling herself
With the long view I hate, telling herself
How foolish it is to expect an indelible place
In hearts open to the rain year after year,
From which the names of spirits finer than hers
Have been washed away, never to be seen again.
Hearts whose bark canoes pull in each evening
At a different dock and unload their tiny cargoes.

Now the truckload of pies scattered in the street
Tempts a crowd of boys from whatever errands
Seemed important a moment ago,
A scene my aunt might use to explain the heart,
How it strays off after novelties.
"Child" is the best label I can hope for
Until I get my chance to explain. Till then
The look of resignation I imagine hers
Seems justified as she sits alone,
Guarding her gift parcels in the waiting room,
The look that says if the gods are patient

Century after century with lazy and thoughtless men,
She can be patient for her little hour.

Worst of all if she's waiting for the train
To take her back, having lumped me with the kind
She warned me years ago not to argue with
The "they" in her sentence "If they block your road
Leave it and walk around, singing your own song."
The "they" in "If they hate the truth,
Don't waste your time trying to be clear."

HISTORY

A shame your students were sullen in class today,
Deaf to the succoring truth of poetry,
Your rare skill at interpreting useless again.
And after school they came with appeals for sympathy
That anyone with a big heart could give them,
Stories of how their fathers have run off,
How their mothers sit in the dark like stones.

Whatever happened at school today
Is only a small part of your story
Like whatever happened elsewhere or will.
And the episodes from my day,
However many there were,
However well I describe them now,
Are fewer than those unaccounted for
That didn't manage to arrive at all.
The nymph Calypso didn't run to meet me
This evening on my walk home.
She didn't offer to share her palmy isle with me
And gladden me forever as a god.
I didn't get the chance to refuse her,
To tell her my place is here with you
In the doomed world. The smell of eggplant
And olive oil when I opened the door
Wasn't as priceless as it might have been.

However true the history of our lives
It can't be relied on, leaving out, as it does,
The generous light we wish to read it by,
Invisible even to the well-intentioned historian
Who may list you, hundreds of years from now,
As an early enlightener of our town,
A woman whose inspired descriptions

Weren't inspired enough to win followers,
Too gentle and vague, they'll say,
To chip away the clay hardening in our ears.

They'll never guess how, after dinner,
As you sat in the dusk of the yard, alone,
I watched you from the porch,
Thinking of the garden you'd entered in your solitude,
How it was hardier than the evening,
How it never will be reconciled to fading under glass
With yesterday and the day before.

VISITING A FRIEND
NEAR SAGAMON HILL

If I take this drive to Sagamon Hill
As leisurely as I can, I may remember,
By the time I spot my friend's house,
My speech of consolation,
Which so far seems to have hidden itself
Among the speeches powerless to console,
The ones that silence would be an improvement on.

The drive over is beautiful,
The road winding through woods with a good smell,
The sunlight filtered and shimmering.
No reason for me to say I'm not one of the lucky ones,
Kin to these towering birch and sycamore,
Lucky like them to have grown on well-drained soil
In unstinted sun, smiled on,
As Homer might say, by Hyperion,
Not like the stunted, scrubby ones
Rooting below in marshland.

Those marsh trees are like my sick friend,
Whose life hasn't been sent to test him
But to sap him, to wear him down.
One life, and he knows that his one hope now
Is to be two people,
The sufferer and the one who observes
His suffering from above
As calmly as Zeus observes from grassy Ida
The armies about Troy,
At ease in the best seat in the house.

That's it, down there, the little dark spot,
Balancing the highlights on the other side.

The scene lingers a moment and then fades.
Zeus drifts back to the clouds;
My friend discovers himself in bed
Listening as a car crunches in the gravel drive,
Hoping that the visitor's cheer
Won't make him gloomy,
That he still wishes the living well.

IV

THE SPANIEL

Piles of leaves at the curb again
And I think of Mitsi, how she loved to flail among them
And burrow in, dooming herself, it turned out,
To a shorter life in the world of cars
Than the life allotted spaniels in general,
However nervous and clumsy the breed may be.

Shrewd of nature to put its money
On the species only, not a penny on the particular.
The odds are good that the blue whale will endure
Unchanged, or changing imperceptibly,
While generations of particular pods
Beached on the bay shore in gales
Are doomed as surely as Mitsi was,
Mitsi who's gone with the sagging front porch
Of the brown and blue house on Granger Street,
The butterfly wallpaper in the front hall,
The bathtub with the fish decals,
The boy I was then, the young man
Who thought he was leaving them all behind.

All lost in the rockslide
While the species holds its place,
Tempting me to believe my deepest nature
The same as the nature of man,
To dismiss the differences,
To ignore the dock hidden among the leaves
Where a boat painted with my colors
Tugs at its chain.
Barely sunrise. No one on the water as I row out.
The brindled spaniel in the bow sleeps quietly,
Not wondering with me if the tide we're riding
Is the one I should have chosen
Or why that cluster of gulls at sundown
Veered off after slowly circling.

THE FAMILY OF MAN

Among all the loons diving in the lake
Not one is diving because it vowed last night
To be truer to its nature, to dive more.
Not one cackles because it believes its father
Would have liked it to
Or reads the half-built lake bridge
As a symbol for the heart's wish for something far
As the fisherman reads it, whose heart has wandered off
While his reason wonders what to do with the twenty
    minutes
That the bridge, when finished, will knock off commut-
    ing time.
And what should he do now as he casts his line
To make the day reveal its meaning?
Not many years left and no reason to believe
This moment will join the list of moments
Certain to endure.
Even the evenings when his father
Carried him piggyback down to the dock
Won't make it there.
What more his father saw in the moonlight
Besides the fish darting in the water
Or heard beneath the hooting of the loons
Is lost now.
Isn't it foolish, the fisherman wonders,
To regret that the boy wasn't more awake,
To believe he'd know all that he'd like to know
If he had begun remembering earlier?

AT BECKY'S PIANO RECITAL

She screws her face up as she nears the hard parts,
Then beams with relief as she makes it through,
Just as she did listening on the edge of her chair
To the children who played before her,
Wincing and smiling for them
As if she doesn't regard them as competitors
And is free of the need to be first
That vexes many all their lives.
I hope she stays like this,
Her windows open on all sides to a breeze
Pungent with sea spray or meadow pollen.
Maybe her patience this morning at the pond
Was another good sign,
The way she waited for the frog to croak again
So she could find its hiding place and admire it.
There it was, in the reeds, to any casual passer-by
Only a fist-sized, speckled stone.
All the way home she wondered out loud
What kind of enemies a frog must have
To make it live so hidden, so disguised.
Whatever enemies follow her when she's grown,
Whatever worry or anger drives her at night from her
    room
To walk in the gusty rain past the town edge,
Her spirit, after an hour, will do what it can
To be distracted by the light of a farmhouse.
What are they doing up there so late,
She'll wonder, then watch in her mind's eye
As the family huddles in the kitchen
To worry if the bank will be satisfied
This month with only half a payment,
If the letter from the wandering son

Really means he's coming home soon.
Even old age won't cramp her
If she loses herself on her evening walk
In piano music drifting from a house
And imagines the upright in the parlor
And the girl working up the same hard passages.

LITTLE LEAGUE

It must be different in the other kingdom in June
When the Little Leaguers are out, screaming in the lots,
And Mr. Dellums, our old coach,
Doesn't have to settle in the outfield
For butterfingers like me or Harvey Schmitz,
For scatter-arms like Jack Montano and Seymour
   Kornfeld,
But can choose his players among the best.
Not called on there to bench boys for catcalls
Or belabor the fundamentals till his voice goes raw.
He should be happy now if fielding an incredible team
Can make him happy. Why he wasted his time with us
Is a mystery. In love with the game, to be sure,
But not, surely, with the way we played it.
Four evenings a week and for no pay.
Maybe he was trying to show his gratitude
To old instructors who put up with his clumsiness.
But how will his heart be tested over there
Where nobody pushes his patience as we did
Past the breaking point? And how will he prove his
   loyalty
To instructors unknown whom fate withheld from him
If every child over there has many teachers to choose
   from,
None forced to dream up some on his own?

ANOTHER ODYSSEUS

Once they listened when I sang the story of Odysseus.
Now the hero they trust,
Too shrewd to believe Penelope still patient,
The swineherd still as loyal as the dog,
Has forgotten Ithaka,
And accepted Kalypso's offer, and become an island god,
Or rules the Phaiacians with young Nausikaä.

And if I persuade them by some miracle
To imagine an Odysseus foolish enough to sneak home,
Cautious in tattered sandals outside his palace,
His sword exchanged for a begging bowl,
They imagine he finds the palace empty,
Wife, son, and swineherd moved off,
Leaving no address.

What good then, they ask, is his famous self-mastery?
What's the point in working up the suspense
To the big moment when he throws his rags off
If there's no one watching but fruit vendors and fishwives
Who think he's a crazy man or a drunk
As he wanders around a town
No more his home than many others,
The name Odysseus itself only another strategy
To be set aside with the others when the time comes?

Now while my Odysseus goes off this morning
With Laertes and Telemachus to prune olive trees,
Should I reason with their Odysseus
As he paces on the dock?
Should I urge him at least to recall his adventures
And ponder the episodes he enjoyed most
And ask what it means to say he handled himself
Better in these than in the others?
Now while the harbor's empty,
Should I urge him to steady himself with comparisons
Before the next story comes sailing in?

THE DIG

Desperate for a peace plan,
They may turn to us one day,
Digging through the debris of sunken cities
Down to our yard, to our brick-lined barbecue,
Which they'll compare to a ruined altar.
What unknown god did we pray to, they'll wonder,
And worry at first it was one of theirs,
Frightened to see how it let its worshipers die away,
Our city nameless, our language lost.

Then, among the few items that didn't rot,
They'll find a child's plastic rake and mower,
Which they'll interpret as tomb gifts,
Miniature tools for our tasks in the underworld.
How we must have enjoyed life, they'll conclude,
If we hoped for no more in the life beyond
Than lawns to be mowed, leaves to be raked,
The same old maples and sycamores.

What ruined a country as peaceful as ours
Was doubtless a warlike country like theirs.
In penance they'll sift through the lumpy mud
For the secret of our tranquil moment.
We must have learned, as we marched to war,
How to drag our feet, how to sail our ships
So slowly they arrived at Troy too late
To be entered in the famous catalogue,
How to sail back, happy to be left out.

Painful to think of those diggers
Trying to work back from our shards
To calm, inviting porches and modest cupolas.
Painful to see them kneeling in the mud,

Carefully piecing a cup together,
Wondering what pledges of loyalty
We sealed with a drink.

No way to reach them with the darker facts.
If we want them to live without illusions
We'll have to carry their dream of us
Back to this life and make it our own.
How long will it take to offer gifts of goodwill
That so far we haven't offered,
To carry out all the promises
That so far we haven't made?

ON THE SOUL

They told you you owned it and you believed them,
Flattered as if a real-estate man,
Pointing to the stone house at the top of the hill
With the nine pillars, had assured you it was yours,
And the dream sounded too good to be resisted,
Even when the doorman had sent you around back,
Even after ten years' work in the kitchen,
Ten years on your bed of straw
Dreaming of the empty suite upstairs
And of the empty bed with the crown
Hanging from the bedpost, bejeweled with your name.

It would have been better if they'd said nothing,
Or told you it lived its own life, like deer
Hidden in the woods, not seen from the road
As you drive past in the car, not seen
When you stop and climb the fence.
Even if they browse on your own land,
They're happiest left alone,
Stepping down in the evening to the stream,
Bedding down in silence under the screen of thickets
To dream what you may guess at and can't know.

THAT POEM

That poem I wrote on the Philippines
When Marcos was stealing his last election
And the protests in Manila seemed to be failing
Was full of a bitterness that sounds contrived now—
A stage speech delivered in black beard and eyebrows
From a courthouse balcony to an empty square.

I should keep the lines tacked to my bulletin board,
A reminder to avoid the marshes of history
And follow the high road of the heart.
At the poem's close, Cory Aquino, gray-haired,
A refugee in New York, loses her voice
At another charity luncheon. Her mouth goes dry
As the eyes of the well-fed audience glaze over,
Though her words about struggling on
Are stirring, if I say so myself, stirring and true,

Truer at least than the speech this evening on the radio
Praising the space shield that will save America,
That's just as reliable as Captain Marvel or Superman.
From war stories like these I should turn inward
To the facts of the heart, should ask what feelings
Need to be nurtured for an ample life.
Wartime and peacetime and still nobody's sure
If the voice of a soul singing to itself
Sounds like the chirp of a cricket
Down in a garden among the bean rows
Or like all the noises in a yard
Going off at once, an orchestra warming up
Or raucous town meeting, with a spirit for every mood.

I wonder if Imelda Marcos enjoyed 400 moods
To fit the famous 400 pairs of shoes

She left behind in the palace when she fled.
Did she choose them the same way Mrs. Aquino chose
Not to accept the offerings of the world
Outside her bedroom window in Manila or Brookline
But to pull her shoes on under a flag
Not yet woven or dyed?

Whose colors I hope she's free now to describe
To rebel leaders in the provinces
Despite the rumbles of unrest at home.
May she mean it when she says both sides
Have to step back from private dreams of power
And listen to the soft voice of reason
Singing its one-line song,
Which should be easy to memorize
Though it hasn't caught on yet
And won't be popular.

THE CIRCUS

If you've done things you should still feel sorry for,
Then sending your check to the Shriner's Circus Fund
For Crippled Children won't make you feel good

Any more than it's made the wife-beater feel good
Or the loan shark or the bookkeeper at the missile plant.
Send it simply, as they do, to sponsor a little joy.

Then if you sit in the crowd you'll wonder
If the crippled children should be laughing with the
    healthy ones
Or shaking their fists at the roof instead with Job's wife,

Refusing to adjust to what they'd never have to adjust to
In a world carefully planned and made.
From your seat in back something will look so wrong

It will dawn on you why the maker was afraid
When Adam and Eve ate from the Tree of Knowledge,
Afraid they'd notice his slipshod craftsmanship.

It won't surprise you then that many aspire to leave,
That the ladder that Plato climbed led him away
From the visible kingdom to a beauty that didn't exist

And never would, that wasn't responsible
For the pitiful imitations. No wonder the couple
On the high trapeze delights the children so much,

Flouting the cloddish law of gravity, trying to be birds.
And then the army of clowns climbing out of the car
That by any law of matter couldn't hold four.

And still they come, another and another,
While those in the crowd who can't jump up
Strain forward in their seats to cheer them on.

TAKING BOTH SIDES

Because they stand back farther, with a wider prospect,
The dead have the advantage in our dialogues,
The words I give them stronger than my own.

First I list my big wishes; then the wishes
I imagine that the dead who know me best
Believe would help me more.

On my list, the wish for a friend
Who'd understand my dreams in terms of the myths
Of sun and moon, sea-beast and healing water.

On their list, the wish I'd listen harder,
My mind less cluttered and small on my lunch hour
When the barber asks for advice about his son.

He's noticed that my thoughts have wandered away
To a place he can't imagine, though the dead can,
The dead I try to keep nothing from.

They know I'm dreaming of a Thebes plagued by a
    question
I alone can answer, of a crowd far livelier
Than the one I enter as I wave the barber good-bye.

The question I want to ask is where should I stand
To enjoy the skyline of my district more,
How near or far, or what should I bring to the dock

For export in the spring when the lake thaws,
What cargo to win the love of the states in the heartland
That years back rushed to join the Union.

The dead wonder when I'm planning to show my
    neighbors
How to love the things I should love now,
Knowing as I do what the dead know.

ON THE WAY TO SCHOOL

Even a lover of the bare truth must admit
This new façade painted on the high-rise
Is a big improvement over the blank face,
Pillars and capitals freshly applied
With a golden pediment and a frieze.
They seem to float above the bare bricks
Like a blurred dream, an admission
Of how much beauty the bricks left out.

Even art that remembers to build beauty in
Has to confine itself to a single theme and exclude
Most of the beautiful truths available,
Even the epic I like to teach each fall
Where the great battle is still raging,
Every hour more proof of how angry Achilles is:
His friends keep losing ground and he still won't help.

What Homer leaves out to concentrate on a war
He points to openly in the similes.
It relieves him to say the battle turns at the hour
When the woodcutter loads his wagon and heads home,
To compare soldiers crowding in for a kill
To summer flies clustering on a milking pail.

When Achilles yields to Priam
And unties the corpse of Hector from his chariot,
He seems to guess that something has been left out
In his quest for glory, as his quest for glory
Reminds me what I miss to rebuff the world.

This morning, on my way to school,
The sun, striking the high-rise head on,
Turns its painted face so shimmery

The illusion takes me in, marble as rich in detail
As the real marble of the city hall
Put up when the romance of commerce and self-rule
Was still strong, Syracuse and Arcade
In friendly competition with Troy and Ithaca,
Doric columns rising a hundred feet from the forest
For a city that didn't exist then and doesn't now.

No details are left out when Homer stops the fighting
For a thousand lines to describe the world
Crowding the face of Achilles' shield.
Here are the two cities in gold relief,
The wedding, the trial in the marketplace,
The harvest and the harvest festival.
Boys and girls dance on the polished dancing floor.
All this Achilles carries on his arm,
Which seems to mean he knows,
When he sees death coming, what life includes,
What exactly death leaves out.

ABOUT THE AUTHOR

Carl Dennis was born in St. Louis in 1939. He now lives in Buffalo, where he teaches in the English Department of the State University of New York. Mr. Dennis is the author of four previous books of poetry: *A House of My Own* (George Braziller, 1974), *Climbing Down* (George Braziller, 1976), *Signs and Wonders* (Princeton University Press, 1979), and *The Near World* (William Morrow, 1985).